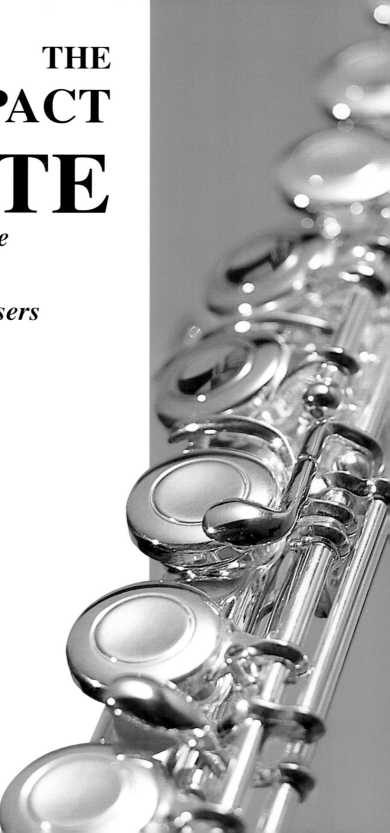

THE
COMPACT
FLUTE

*A complete guide
to the flute and
ten great composers*

written by
Barrie Carson Turner

MACMILLAN

First published 1996 by Macmillan Children's Books
a division of Macmillan Publishers Limited
25 Eccleston Place, London SW1W 9NF
and Basingstoke

Associated companies throughout the world

ISBN 0 333 64033 0

9 8 7 6 5 4 3 2 1

A CIP catalogue record for this book is available from the British Library.

Typeset by Macmillan Children's Books
Colour repro by Track QSP Ltd.
Printed in Singapore

Text written by Barrie Carson Turner

Designer: Nigel Davies
Commissioning Editor: Susie Gibbs
Art Director: Anne Glenn
CD Consultant: Tony Locantro
Picture Researcher: Josine Meijer
Project Editor: Jane Robertson

Contents

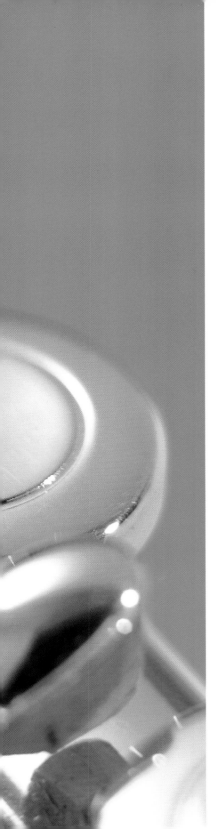

OVERTURE

Playing and listening to music, as well as learning about it, is one of the most popular and exciting pastimes in the world today.

The flute is an extremely ancient instrument, dating back to the Stone Age. The first flutes were not played for enjoyment, but their whistling sounds were used to frighten away enemies or evil spirits, or to act as signalling devices. Our modern flute is called the 'transverse' or 'cross' flute because it is played and held crossways, while earlier flutes were held straight out in front of the player, like today's recorder.

In eighteenth-century Europe, fashion demanded music that was pleasing to listen to, highly melodic, and lightly accompanied. Composers discovered that the flute, remodelled and improved, fitted these demands perfectly. Often composers were players themselves and, because fashionable society wanted to learn the instrument, many players were also teachers.

Today, orchestras have at least two flutes, one flautist often also playing the piccolo (the smallest flute of all). In the twentieth century the flute has made a comeback as a solo instrument, and composers have once more started to write challenging works for it.

The flute is important in many cultures, and in this book you will see different examples of flutes from around the world. In Japan, the ancient *shakuhachi* was once played by wandering monks who, it is said, also used the instrument as a means of self-defence! The *panpipes* are played on every continent in the world, and are known to have existed for 4,000 years.

The modern flute is made of metal, either alloy or silver, or sometimes stainless steel; but makers have occasionally also made instruments from precious metals such as gold or platinum. On pages 18 and 19 you will see photographs of a modern flute maker's workshop. Each stage of the construction of the flute requires great expertise and close attention to detail.

The audio compact disc from EMI features extracts of music written by each of the ten composers in the book. The short section *On the CD*, which appears in the text for each composer, tells you a little about the music.

Whether you are already a flautist, just beginning lessons or simply interested in flute playing, *The Compact Flute* will add to the range of your knowledge and understanding of the flute.

THE FLUTE FAMILY

Piccolo

Like its larger relation the flute, the piccolo can be made from metal or wood, or a combination of both. Occasionally it is made from silver or even gold. It is half the size of the ordinary flute and sounds an octave higher. Vivaldi was one of the first composers to write for the piccolo but it was Beethoven who first introduced the piccolo into the modern orchestra by scoring it in his Fifth and Sixth Symphonies.

The piccolo is the smallest instrument in the modern flute family (piccolo is Italian for 'small'). It is also the highest instrument used in the orchestra today. The shrill sound of the piccolo can be heard above the largest orchestra playing at its loudest.

Played in its higher register the flute becomes an extremely powerful instrument capable of holding its own among other instruments. The low notes of the flute are truly rich and smooth, and have been used by many composers for special orchestral effects.

Flute

The flute is one of the most important members of the modern orchestra. It is an extremely versatile instrument – its soft, smooth tones combining easily with strings, piano and other woodwind instruments. At the same time it is an ideal instrument for playing in small instrumental combinations or intimate

Although the flute was well established in the orchestra by the nineteenth century, composers did not often write for it as a solo instrument. During the twentieth century, however, the flute's repertoire has expanded remarkably, as modern composers have discovered its powerful and artistic solo capabilities.

Alto flute

The Italian word *alto* means 'high', but when used with reference to instruments it usually indicates middle pitch. The alto flute is a slightly deeper and larger version of the usual flute, and its sound is accordingly fuller and richer. Its lowest note is identical in pitch to the violin's G string.

A variation of the alto flute is the *flute d'amour*. This flute was popular in the eighteenth century when it was used for low register playing.

Right: Alto flute with curved headjoint. The alto flute was invented by the great flute and instrument maker, Theobald Boehm, 'the father of the modern flute'. He transcribed many pieces for the instrument, and promoted its popularity.

Far right: Alto flute with straight headjoint.

Bass flute

The earliest bass flute dates back over 400 years, although the first practical design did not appear until the early years of the twentieth century. This curious instrument was shaped like the letter T, with the larger length of tubing held vertically, while the mouthpiece was situated in the crossbar.

Right: The bass flute is the lowest member of the flute family and sounds an octave below the orchestral flute. Modern flute makers have added a bend in the tube. A bracket and stem attachment allows the instrument to rest on the player's right leg.

WIND INSTRUMENTS AROUND THE WORLD

Dvojnice (*Croatia*)
The Croatian dvojnice is cleverly carved from a single block of wood, and traditionally played by shepherds. The two pipes can also be played separately. The player sometimes holds the instrument at one side of the mouth so that one pipe receives more air, and sounds louder.

Zampoña (*Ecuador*)
The zampoña are panpipes from the Andes of South America. The instrument is made up of a set of vertical pipes, tied together. Each pipe sounds only one note. Players blow across the tops of the tubes to make a pleasant whistling sound. Panpipes are known to have existed for 4,000 years, and are played in every continent of the world.

Nāy (*Egypt*)
The nāy is a very old flute which was once played by the ancient Egyptians. It is held in the side of the mouth, the player blowing across the top edge of the instrument. A skilled nāy player can produce a scale of three octaves. 'Nāy' comes from an old Persian word meaning 'reed'.

Shakuhachi *(Japan)*
In the sixteenth century the Japanese shakuhachi was played by wandering monks, once *samurai*, who begged and lived a life of poverty. It is said that the instrument was used as a means of self-defence, as well as music-making! The shakuhachi is still very important in Japanese art and folk music today.

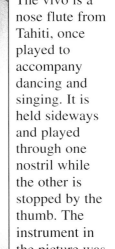

Vivo *(Tahiti)*
The vivo is a nose flute from Tahiti, once played to accompany dancing and singing. It is held sideways and played through one nostril while the other is stopped by the thumb. The instrument in the picture was collected during Captain Cook's first voyage.

Kooauau *(New Zealand)*
The kooauau, played by the Maori people of New Zealand, is a small flute about 12cm long. It is blown from the end and has only three finger holes. It is made of wood or bone which is often elaborately carved. The kooauau is commonly worn as an ornament when not in use.

INSTRUMENTAL GROUPS

Music for solo flute

Composers seldom write for solo unaccompanied 'melody' instruments (instruments like the flute that can only play one line of music at once). This is because two players are 'easier' to listen to than one, and an accompaniment allows a soloist to take an occasional few bars' rest. Writing for an unaccompanied instrument is very difficult, and requires a keen musical imagination. Bach wrote two solo flute sonatas and there are also works by other eighteenth-century composers including Telemann and Quantz.

Flute and keyboard

Woodwind instruments like the flute blend well with the keyboard, and composers have written a variety of works for this combination of instruments. There are many sonatas for flute and harpsichord by eighteenth-century composers, as well as sets of variations, including Schubert's variations for flute and piano on his own song 'Withered Flowers'. During the twentieth century many composers have once again become interested in writing for flute and piano.

Flute duets

A duet is a piece for two performers. In the eighteenth century, when flute playing was one of the most popular pastimes of the wealthy, composers were keen to supply easy pieces for the amateur flautist. Today duets are still popular with flautists. Some duets are specifically written as learning pieces.

Flute trios and quartets

A trio is a piece for three instruments, and a quartet is for four instruments. The flute associates well with other instruments, and flute trios and quartets have been written for a variety of combinations of instruments. Mozart wrote four 'flute quartets' – not for four flutes but for one flute and strings! Haydn's 'flute trios' are for two flutes and cello. The German composer Friedrich Kuhlau has written several trios and quartets for three and four flutes.

Flute concertos

The word 'concerto' was simply used to describe a performance 'together'. Over the last 250 years, however, it has come to mean a composition for one solo instrument and orchestra. Many flute concertos were written during the heyday of the instrument in the eighteenth century – virtuoso players constantly needed new pieces to play.

The flute in the orchestra

At the beginning of the nineteenth century composers no longer found the quiet tone of the flute appropriate to their needs. Public concerts were growing more frequent, concert halls were growing in size, and the flute as a solo instrument fell out of fashion with composers. The flute remained an essential part of the orchestra, however, and was given its own share of important solos to play.

The flute in the twentieth century

At the beginning of the twentieth century composers such as Debussy rediscovered the solo possibilities of the flute. The French composer Jacques Ibert contributed a flute concerto to the flute's growing new repertoire, and several mainstream composers such as Poulenc wrote flute sonatas. Ravel included the flute in his chamber music and more recently composers such as John Cage have written flute music which expands the technique of the instrument.

THE HISTORY OF THE FLUTE

Diſcantus.

Altus.

Tenor.

Baſſus.

Early flutes were made in several different sizes, like the descant, alto, tenor and bass instruments in this illustration of 1545.

Early flutes

The flute is an extremely ancient instrument, dating back to the Stone Age. The earliest musical instruments were used to frighten away enemies or evil spirits, or to act as signalling devices.

Flutes have also been associated with hunting, and used as 'decoys' to imitate the sound of an animal or bird. Decoy flutes are still used today.

Early European flutes were 'end-blown' – that is, played like today's recorder; our modern flute is called the 'transverse' or

A shepherd plays a transverse flute in this eleventh-century manuscript painting.

'cross' flute because it is held crossways in front of the player. We know the transverse flute was played in China three thousand years ago, but it may date from even earlier. The instrument first appeared in Europe nine hundred years ago when a small version of it was adopted by the military, and later named the fife.

An illustration from Jacques Hotteterre's first manual on flute playing, showing a one-keyed conical flute.

Above: During the sixteenth century the popularity of the transverse flute grew immensely with amateurs as well as professional players.

Below: An early instruction manual for the recorder. The recorder was called the flute à bec (beaked flute) because of the beak-like shape of the mouthpiece.

The Hotteterre Family

In France during the second half of the seventeenth century a family of instrument makers called Hotteterre remodelled and improved many of the woodwind instruments of the period, including the transverse flute. The new flute was made in three short sections or 'joints'. The player could 'fine tune' the instrument by pushing in or pulling out the head joint. The positioning of the finger holes was adjusted, bringing them closer together and within easier reach of the hand, and a 'key' was added to improve access to the furthest hole.

The transverse flute

The tone of the transverse flute was more powerful than that of the recorder, which meant it balanced better with the new, bigger and louder orchestras of the period.

A new school of flute virtuosi appeared, many of them associated with the French court where flute playing had always been fashionable. In 1752 the composer and flautist Johann Joachim Quantz published a comprehensive guide to the flute, including his own thoughts on the theory of flute playing and teaching, as well as the history of the instrument.

Right: The flute has often featured in traditional folk-tales, such as that of the Pied Piper of Hamelin, who rid the town of rats by charming them with his flute playing.

Below: The Fifer by the French painter Manet. The foot soldiers' fife, a tiny flute similar to the piccolo, was first played in Germany and Switzerland.

Corps de rechange

Today, music pitch is the same throughout the world, but at the beginning of the eighteenth century, pitch varied from town to town and even between orchestras. Flautists were not able to alter the pitch of their instruments, so instrument makers redesigned the flute in *four* sections, providing one section with interchangeable alternative sections of various lengths. Fitting a longer section made the instrument longer and lowered the pitch, while fitting a shorter section raised the pitch. These alternative sections were called by their French name, *corps de rechange*.

But the flute still had faults which late-eighteenth-century makers were determined to rectify. Certain notes, for instance, were still out of tune, often because the precise place for the finger hole was still too far away for the fingers to reach it conveniently. Further keys were added to try and improve this situation. By the turn of the century the instrument was ready for its final transformation by the flute maker Theobald Boehm.

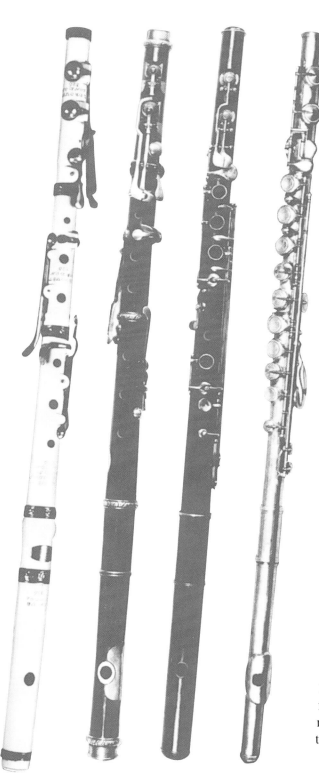

Nineteenth- and twentieth-century flutes. Second from the left is an instrument modelled on the flute played by the British virtuoso, Charles Nicholson.

Theobald Boehm

Theobald Boehm began life as a goldsmith and jeweller, but soon found himself more attracted to a musical career as a flautist and flute maker. By 1828 he had established an instrument-making workshop and had begun work on his own ideas to rebuild the flute. Boehm visited London in 1831 and was impressed by the flute playing of the London virtuoso Charles Nicholson. Nicholson's flute had very wide finger holes, which produced a powerful tone. Boehm incorporated larger finger holes into his new design and added an improved mechanism. In 1832 he introduced his finished flute to the musical world. Within ten years he had licensed the manufacture of his instrument to makers in Paris and London.

In 1846, Boehm set about reworking and perfecting his designs, aiming at further improvements. The new flute was not an immediate success, although flute players slowly accepted it. Except for several minor modifications, the Boehm flute remains the standard model in use today.

15

HOW THE FLUTE WORKS

Wind instruments, like the flute, produce their sound from a vibrating column of air inside a hollow body. The player blows against the sharp edge of the mouthpiece, which interrupts the stream of air, setting up a series of vibrations which are modified and amplified by the instrument. Sound is produced when the vibrations reach the listener's ear.

The length of a tube (the body of the instrument) controls the pitch – a long tube will produce low notes, and a short tube high notes. Opening a finger hole will shorten the tube by allowing the air to escape earlier, and so the note will be higher. By opening the finger holes in preset patterns, a scale can be obtained. The player blows harder and adjusts the embouchure – the playing position of the lips - to obtain notes at a higher octave.

The **keywork** of the flute looks very complicated, but is designed to make the instrument much easier to play.

A **pad** below each key ensures an air-tight fit with the raised rim of the hole.

Tiny **springs** ensure the keys return to their resting position after they are released.

The flute is open at this end.

Fingers press the **keys** to cover the holes. Some keys are coupled to others and are activated automatically when another key is pressed or released.

The **middle joint** contains most of the keywork.

The **foot joint** carries the keys for the right-hand little finger.

The modern flute is made in three sections or 'joints', which fit together very tightly to ensure there is no leakage of air which would affect the tone of the instrument.

The **head joint** can be pulled out to adjust the tuning (the pitch) of the instrument.

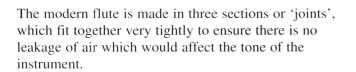

Players rest the flute on the side of the left hand, where the finger joins the hand.

The flute is closed with a plug or stopper that can be adjusted to assist tuning.

Blow-hole. The player's breath is directed against the sharp edge.

The **lip-plate** is shaped to allow the player's lips to rest comfortably against the instrument and to direct the player's breath against the blow-hole at the correct angle.

Soundwave of a flute note

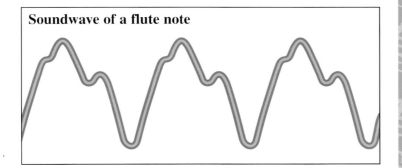

The mechanism of the flute consists of an ingenious system of linked and extended keys.

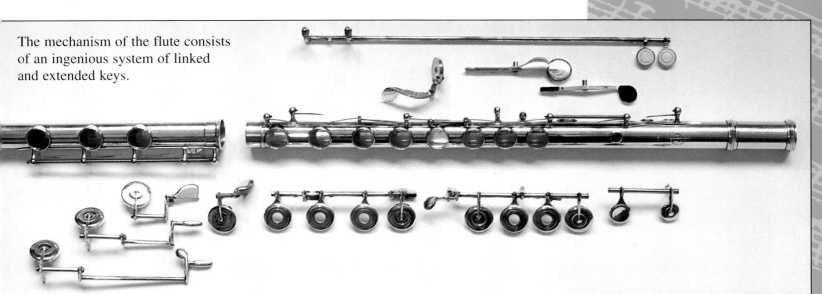

HOW THE FLUTE IS MADE

The modern flute is made of metal, usually alloy or silver, or sometimes stainless steel. Occasionally makers have used precious metals such as gold or platinum. The harder the metal, the brighter the instrument sounds, and so a soft metal like gold will produce a slightly duller sound.

The metal flute has many advantages over the old wooden instrument. It allows the player more control over tone quality and it has a superb upper register.

Components required to make a flute **key**. The mechanical workings of the flute must be reliable and responsive to the player's touch, and every detail of construction must be perfect.

Below: The flute maker at his workbench. Making a flute requires great expertise and close attention to detail.

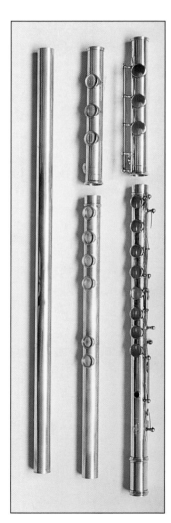

On a modern metal flute the **mouthpiece** must be raised above the thin metal body of the instrument. This imitates the thickness of the wood on an original wooden instrument, and is essential for good sound quality.

The construction of the **middle joint** and the **foot joint**. The tone holes are soldered onto the metal tube, and the centres are then removed.

Modern equipment has made the instrument maker's task easier and quicker, although no less skilled.

The instrument is finished and ready to leave the maker's workshop.

Precision tools are an important part of the flute maker's kit. Many of the hand tools used today are based on traditional designs dating back many years.

Detailed final adjustments are made to the keywork.

HOW THE FLUTE IS PLAYED

The light and airy tone of the newly remodelled flute lent itself ideally to performing the elegant music of the eighteenth century. As the century progressed and further improvements were made, virtuoso performers expanded their playing techniques, and with the flute's acceptance as a full member of the orchestra the demand for flutes increased. In the twentieth century the flute has taken its place among the foremost virtuoso and orchestral instruments.

Tonguing

Flute players 'tongue' a note by saying 'te' or 'de' as they play. This causes the tongue to flick back to the roof of the mouth, bringing about a quick release of air, which is directed into the instrument. 'Tonguing' ensures that notes begin with precision and crispness.

Fluttertonguing

If a flautist rolls a letter R while playing, the notes produced will have a curious purring or buzzing sound.

Phrasing

A 'phrase' is like a musical sentence, and gives music shape and expression. Flute players phrase or 'slur' notes by joining them together smoothly in one breath. In written music phrases are indicated by curved lines.

Staccato playing

The Italian word staccato means 'detached'. In flute playing, staccato notes are all tongued separately. The use of a certain amount of staccato adds elegance to playing; rapid staccato is often employed for light, bouncy tunes.

Tremolo

This Italian word means 'trembling'. To flute players, tremolo means playing two alternate notes in rapid succession. Played low down in the flute's range, the effect can sound mysterious and almost sinister, and when played high up it sounds shrill and frightening.

Playing low notes

The sound of the flute playing in the lowest part of its register is warm and mellow. It is sometimes compared with a trumpet playing softly. Several composers have written for the flute in this way, especially Debussy.

Playing high notes

The sound of the flute playing high notes is powerful and strong. Composers often give the flute the same notes as the violins, but an octave higher. The highest notes in the flute's range require a great deal of breath, and can only be played loud.

As with most instruments, correct fingering of notes is an essential part of good flute playing.

Vibrato

The effect of vibrato is like a gentle wavering in the sound of each note. It adds richness to a player's tone.

The flute is taken apart for travelling, and fitted into a heavily padded case which holds each joint firmly.

All wind instruments suffer from condensation inside the tube. It is important that any moisture remaining in the instrument after playing is wiped away as soon as possible. For this purpose a 'pull-through' cloth is used.

VIVALDI
1678–1741

Throughout his long life Antonio Vivaldi was a prolific composer, although only about a fifth of his compositions was published in his lifetime. He was the first composer to write specifically for the new 'transverse' flute.

Right: *Transverse flute, c.1723.*

It was clear to Vivaldi's father, Giovanni, himself a professional violinist, that his young son had a natural gift for music. At the first opportunity, Antonio was sent to study at the famous cathedral of St Mark's in Venice.

Vivaldi was always interested in new developments in music. He was particularly interested when he first heard the transverse or 'cross' flute, an instrument rarely played at the time. During Vivaldi's lifetime the transverse flute quickly gained in popularity, rapidly replacing its cousin, the recorder.

In 1703 Vivaldi joined the staff of the most respected music conservatory in Venice, the Ospedale della Pietà. There he remained for most of his life, writing a number of flute works for performance by the students. Vivaldi composed music for private as well as public performance. It is likely that most of his solo sonatas, including four for flute, were written as private commissions. From 1723 the governors at the Ospedale commissioned Vivaldi to write two new concertos every month.

In 1728 Vivaldi published a set of six concertos for flute and strings – the very first concertos for this combination of instruments. Several of the works were new arrangements of previous pieces written for the now unfashionable recorder.

Finger positions for playing the recorder. In Vivaldi's day 'flute' usually meant recorder.

Vivaldi occasionally gave his works descriptive titles. He called the first concerto in the 1728 set *La tempesta di mare* ('The Storm at Sea'), and another work, *Il gardellino* ('The Goldfinch'). In both these pieces Vivaldi tried to create the sounds suggested by the titles.

Vivaldi wrote thirteen concertos for flute and string orchestra. The idea of a 'concerto' – today usually a piece for one solo instrument and orchestra – was very new in Vivaldi's time. He did much to establish the three-movement pattern of the concerto which is still popular today.

This caricature of Vivaldi was drawn in 1723 by the Italian painter Pier Leone Ghezzi, who achieved fame through his caricatures of influential and famous people.

ON THE CD
Flute Concerto in G minor ('La Notte') Op.10 No.2
I. Largo – Presto (Fantasmi) II. Presto III. Largo (Il sonno) IV. Allegro

Vivaldi wrote this concerto for performance by the orchestra of the music academy where he taught. The flute part is particularly difficult, and contains much 'display work', allowing soloists to show off their skills. Two of the movements have secondary titles: *Fantasmi* ('Phantoms') has fiery music, and *Il sonno* ('The Sleep') has music which is appropriately slow and ponderous.

TELEMANN

1681–1767

George Philipp Telemann was one of the most respected composers of his day. His admirers included both Handel and Bach (who asked him to be the godfather of one of his sons).

By the age of ten Telemann had begun composing, and could play several instruments competently, including the violin and the flute. He improved his knowledge of instruments by attending orchestral concerts, and at the age of twenty entered Leipzig University. Telemann only completed one year of study, after which he left to begin his career in music.

While at university, Telemann founded an amateur music group, the collegium musicum ('music society'), the first of many such groups he was to direct during his long life. Much of the chamber music Telemann wrote for this and similar groups featured flutes, oboes and strings. The music is written in *style galant* ('elegant style'), meaning it is highly decorated with trills, turns, and other ornaments.

The flute of Telemann's day was still a relatively soft-sounding instrument, and was particularly appropriate for playing in small instrumental groups. Telemann wrote one hundred 'trio sonatas', a piece for two solo instruments and accompaniment which was popular at the time, as well as sonatas for flute. More unusual are the series of duets he wrote for two flutes.

Some of Telemann's most well-known music is found in the three collections of *Musique de table*. This French title simply means 'Table Music'. It was used by Telemann and other composers to describe music written for performance during dinner at important state or private functions. The flute features regularly in these works, its soft unobtrusive tone making it ideal for background entertainment.

Concerts were as popular in Telemann's time as they are today. They varied from small local events to grand spectacular displays such as the concert featured here.

It was in coffee houses such as this that Telemann met and rehearsed his groups of student musicians. Amateur music groups in Germany were very popular at the time.

In 1740, when Telemann was at the height of his career, he stopped composing to give more time to writing about music. For the next fifteen years he composed virtually nothing. However, in 1755 his lifelong friend Handel persuaded him to start composing again, which he did until his death twelve years later.

George Frideric Handel, who greatly admired Telemann's skills as a composer. Handel once said Telemann could write an eight-part mass as easily as other people could write a letter.

The first page of an instrumental composition by Telemann, written at the age of eighty-six, in the last year of his life.

J. S. BACH

1685–1750

During Johann Sebastian Bach's middle years the flute gradually established itself in the orchestra. At first it played the same music as the lead violins (usually an octave higher to give the music an extra brightness), but soon composers began to treat it as an instrument in its own right, and gave it important solos.

J. S. Bach was born into what was probably the largest family of musicians in music history. The Bach family can be traced back to the sixteenth century.

Bach's first flute music was the result of a valuable commission from the Margrave of Brandenburg, an important member of the nobility and a keen amateur musician. Bach wrote six works for the Margrave, which today we know as the Brandenburg Concertos. The flute features as one of the solo instruments in the fifth concerto. Bach also includes the flute in his 'triple concerto', which uses music taken and rearranged from several of his earlier works.

The title page of Bach's Brandenburg Concertos. Bach included a very elegant dedication letter in French when he sent the finished manuscript to the Margrave.

Left: *The Brandenburg Gate in Berlin, 1825.*

Bach wrote two sonatas for flute and harpsichord and two further sonatas for flute and basso continuo. This term simply means 'accompaniment'. However, only directions for the accompanying chords are given. It is left to the performer to compose their own accompaniment from these directions.

Bach also wrote an unaccompanied sonata for flute. Unaccompanied works are probably the most difficult pieces of all to compose. In order to maintain interest for the listener, the soloist must play almost all the time – as the only alternative is silence.

ON THE CD
***Orchestral Suite No. 2
in B minor BWV 1067
Badinerie***

Bach's suite opens with the customary stately Overture, which is followed by seven dance movements of which *Badinerie* is the last. The flute has often been associated with dancing, and in this suite Bach has written bright, airy music for it.

The Margrave Christian Ludwig of Brandenburg who commissioned Bach's six Brandenburg Concertos.

Bach also included the flute in his church cantatas and large choral works, often writing beautiful solo passages for the instrument, which weave in and out of the singer's melody. One such piece is the flute part to 'In love my Saviour now is dying' from the *St Matthew Passion*. Other beautiful music written by Bach for flute can be found in the 'Pastorale' of the *Christmas Oratorio*, where the flute represents the shepherds, and the strings the angels.

Left: *In the first half of the eighteenth century the flute became popular with amateur players. It was a conveniently small instrument for carrying, and could be played anywhere.*

Right: *The flute, with its peaceful and tranquil tone, has traditionally been associated with shepherds and pastoral scenes.*

HANDEL
1685–1759

When George Frideric Handel moved to London the transverse flute was already a popular instrument. It was played and enjoyed in the home, and heard often at concerts.

Handel made two visits to London, in 1711 and 1712, where his works were so successful that he decided to live in England permanently. During the composer's early years in London, the modern transverse flute was rapidly replacing the recorder. The tone of the recorder was now too soft to compete with the increasing size of the orchestra, and especially the powerful sound of the new violin family. At the same time the flute had also undergone improvements, and now had a wider pitch range.

Handel's most important works for flute are his sonatas. They have grand French titles: *Douze sonatas pour une traversière, un violon ou hautbois con basse-continue* (twelve sonatas for flute, violin, or oboe, with basso continuo). Although orchestral music often did not include parts for flutes, it was accepted that flutes, if available, played the oboe line.

Handel wrote almost forty operas, and many other choral works. He often scored for flute in his operas; in *Rinaldo* he cleverly uses a tiny flute to represent the sound of birds.

Left: *Vauxhall Gardens, London. These famous pleasure gardens on the south side of the river Thames at Lambeth were a popular concert venue.*

Right: *Handel's house: 25 Brook Street, London.*

Handel's most well-known composition is probably the *Water Music*, first performed on 17 July 1717 for George I at a splendid water pageant on the Thames in London. Handel wrote the music in three parts or 'suites'. Two suites include brass, instruments traditionally associated with outdoor music. But for the third suite Handel has chosen the more peaceful sounds of flutes, recorder, strings and bassoons. When the *Water Music* was later published Handel included an arrangement for flute, especially for the flute-playing British market.

ON THE CD
Concerto Grosso in G
Op.3 No.3
I. Largo e staccato II. Allegro
III. Adagio IV. Allegro

Handel probably wrote his Opus 3 set of concertos (his first music in this style) while employed by the Duke of Chandos. The works were inspired by the concertos of Handel's older contemporary Arcangelo Corelli.

Below: The first page of Handel's manuscript of the Water Music. King George was so pleased with Handel's music that he asked for it to be repeated three times.

Below: George I and Handel during the performance of the Water Music. The royal party travelled by boat from Westminster to Chelsea where a magnificent supper had been prepared.

QUANTZ

1697–1773

Johann Joachim Quantz, one of the most famous flautists and flute composers of his day, began his career as an oboist, and only later took up the flute. Throughout his varied life he worked as a composer, flautist, flute maker, teacher, music director and writer.

Stanislas Lesczinski, King of Poland. Quantz played in the King's orchestra as a young man.

Quantz was born in Germany, and as a child played several instruments competently. In his late teens he lodged in Dresden, where he came into contact with local music-making. After a period of travel and study in Vienna he returned to Dresden and took up a post of oboe player in the orchestra of the King of Poland. It was at this time that he began flute lessons with the great player and teacher, Buffardin.

In 1728, during a visit to Berlin, his flute-playing attracted the attention of the amateur flautist and patron of the arts, the young Prince Frederick of Prussia. The Prince invited Quantz to become his flute teacher. Quantz accepted, and from this time a lifelong friendship and musical association developed between the two men. On his accession to the throne in 1740 Frederick expanded the musical retinue of the Court at Potsdam and appointed Quantz as chamber musician and court composer.

Quantz composed prolifically, writing an immense amount of flute music for performance by the King and his court musicians. Two hundred flute sonatas, sixty sonatas for flute and other instruments, about three hundred flute concertos, and many other smaller works appeared over the next thirty years. Quantz continued composing right up until his death in 1773.

Above: Dresden, where Quantz lived as a young man. He heard Vivaldi's concertos here, and as a composer was very much influenced by them.

Left: *Frederick's magnificent palace at Potsdam, near Berlin. The King's household included many of the finest musicians in Europe.*

Left: *King Frederick the Great playing the flute.*

ON THE CD
Concerto in E minor for flute and string orchestra
II. Affettuoso

The Concerto in E minor is composed in the ornate 'gallant' style fashionable in Quantz's day. The directions to the player were written in a musical 'short hand', but performers were free to add their own ornamentation where appropriate.

Fingering instructions for playing the flute from Quantz's How to play the transverse flute, *published in 1752, and dedicated to his patron, Frederick.*

Quantz also improved the mechanism of the flute. He fitted a tuning slide into the head joint of the instrument (this idea is still in use today) and he added an extra key on the lowest part of the body of the instrument to give an additional note and improve the tuning of several others.

While composing indefatigably for the flute, Quantz was also drawing together his own thoughts on the theory of flute-playing and teaching, and in 1752 he published a great treatise on the flute.

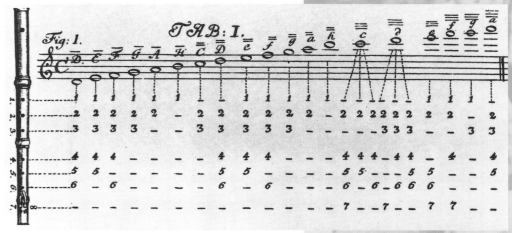

J. C. BACH

1735–1782

We do not know much about J. C. Bach's childhood, but with the great Johann Sebastian as his father he is almost certain to have studied at home. On his father's death, his half-brother Carl Philipp Emanuel Bach supervised the boy's studies. It was then that Johann Christian composed his first pieces.

Bach's real success as a composer began in London. He moved to England in 1762 in response to a commission to write two operas. Although no further opera work was forthcoming, he decided to stay in London, and lived there for the rest of his life. Soon he was a regular visitor at the court of George III and Queen Charlotte. King George played the flute, and Bach was offered a position as 'court chamber musician'.

Johann Christian Bach was the youngest son of J. S. Bach and his second wife Anna Magdalena. He was known as the 'English Bach' because of his life spent in London. The flute plays an important part in his chamber music.

A grand concert in Bologna. As a young composer Bach studied at Bologna with the great teacher Padre Giovanni Battista Martini.

Left: George III arriving at the palace at Hampton Court, by the artist Thomas Rowlandson. Bach was 'royal music master' to the King.

During his first year in London Bach met the bass viol player and composer Carl Friedrich Abel, who had studied with Bach's father. Their friendship soon turned into a fruitful business venture. Over a period of twenty years they established an important series of public concerts. Bach's 'Six Grand Overtures' were performed in 1781. Three of the pieces are for 'double orchestra' – one orchestra is made up of strings, oboes, bassoons and horns, while the other uses the more gentle combination of strings and flutes for an 'echo' effect.

Bach wrote chamber music throughout his life, often on commission, or for performance at court chamber music concerts. His sonatas were greatly

ON THE CD
Quintet in D for flute, oboe, violin, viola and cello Op.11 No.6
I. Allegro II. Andantino
III. Allegro assai

J. C. Bach's first major chamber music work to include flutes is the set of six quintets for flute, oboe, violin, viola and cello accompaniment. Following the success of this work Bach wrote further quintets, quartets and trios.

respected by Leopold Mozart who, with his eight-year-old son Wolfgang, met Bach in London. Although Bach was one of the foremost composers of his day, within a few short years of his death his name was almost forgotten, and his music suddenly was no longer fashionable.

Below: Carl Friedrich Abel (1723–1787). Both Bach and Abel wrote music for their regular concerts at the Hanover Square Rooms, and performed there.

C. F. ABEL.

Left: The Hanover Square Rooms, a popular concert venue for almost a century. Bach and Abel both contributed money for the construction of the building.

C. STAMITZ
1745–1801

Johann Stamitz, father of Carl, and first Music Director of the Mannheim orchestra. When Johann died at the age of only thirty-nine Carl's music lessons were taken over by other players in the famous orchestra.

François-Joseph Gossec, composer and one of the directors of the Concert Spirituel who Stamitz met in Paris.

The palace at Mannheim where the Elector Carl Theodor brought together the finest composers and musicians to serve in his household.

The father of Carl Stamitz, Johann Stamitz, was also a composer, and gave his son his first music lessons. By the age of seventeen Carl was playing second violin in the orchestra, an ideal situation from which to learn about instruments and their music.

In 1770 he left Germany to seek a new life in Paris, where he became court composer to Duke Louis of Noailles. In this prestigious position he met many other great musicians, and had his first chance to earn a living through his composing. He found that flute-playing in Paris was one of the most fashionable pastimes of the day.

Stamitz wrote concertos for a variety of solo instruments. Among the many works of this kind are seven pieces for flute. One work is written for an amazing seven solo instruments with orchestra – flute, oboe, clarinet, two horns, violin and cello. Stamitz's concertos were very popular with Parisian audiences, and many were performed at the celebrated annual series of concerts known as the Concert Spirituel.

In London, Stamitz found few problems in selling his compositions. Chamber music in particular was in demand for the many amateur flautists in London musical society. It was not long before Stamitz had published a series of duets and sonatas for the flute. But Stamitz's success and fame in the early part of his career did not survive much beyond middle age. He died at the age of fifty-six with enormous debts.

Christian Cannabich, Stamitz's successor as chamber director at Mannheim and Munich.

The title page of the Grand Overture in the composer's hand. 'God Save the King' was written in 1791 by Stamitz, and signed 'Charles' as he liked to be known in England.

In the summer months elegant parties always included music as entertainment, and it is likely Stamitz's own chamber compositions were put to this use.

ON THE CD
Flute Concerto in G
Op.29 I. Allegro

It is thought that as many as four flute concertos by Stamitz have been lost. The Concerto in G dates from Stamitz's years in Paris, when he was earning a princely income from the publication and performance of his compositions.

MOZART
1756–1791

Leopold Mozart was delighted when his son Wolfgang Amadeus first began to show an interest in music. Although Mozart claimed the flute was far from his favourite instrument (the piano was probably this) it features in all his mature orchestral works, and in many solo pieces.

Leopold Mozart (1719–1787) composer and violinist, Mozart's father and his first music teacher.

Mozart wrote his first music for the flute – six sonatas – when he was only eight and living in London. Leopold, Wolfgang, and his sister Nannerl lived in London for over a year, from April 1764 to July 1765 and received great hospitality from King George III.

The flute, or 'German' flute as it was called in England, had been extremely popular in London since Handel's day. However, it was not until the middle of Mozart's life that the instrument became fully accepted into the orchestra. All Mozart's later orchestral works include flutes.
In December 1777

The impressive wedding of Joseph II and Isabella at the palace of Schönbrunn in 1760 was watched by the four-year-old Mozart.

Wolfgang sent a letter to his father telling him he had received a commission to write several flute works for the Dutch flautist Monsieur de Jean. Mozart wrote two concertos the following year. Unfortunately de Jean did not like one of the slow movements of the concertos. Mozart could not afford to lose the friendship of a valuable patron, and so without argument wrote a replacement movement. Mozart kept the rejected movement and it has survived, and is still played by flautists today. The composer also wrote three flute quartets (pieces for flute and strings) for de Jean, this time without incident.

In 1778 Mozart was living in Paris, seeking commissions and performing work, as well as looking for new pupils. Business seemed poor, and many of the nobility he and his father had met when Wolfgang was a child no longer seemed interested in Mozart the adult. However, one particular nobleman, the Count of Guines, was interested. The Count was an amateur

ON THE CD
Concerto in C for flute and harp K299
II. Andantino

Although the flute was not Mozart's favourite instrument, this clearly did not restrict his writing beautiful music for it. The concerto for flute and harp is full of graceful melodies suited to the delicate tones of the solo instruments.

flute player, and his daughter played the harp, so he commissioned Mozart to write a concerto for both instruments, the Concerto in C for flute and harp.

In 1791, the final year of his life, Mozart wrote his most famous opera, *The Magic Flute*. In the story, the magic flute is given to the hero, Prince Tamino, who by playing it keeps himself from harm. In no other work by any other composer is the flute given such importance.

In the same year, Mozart wrote his Adagio and Rondo for glass harmonica, flute, oboe, viola, and cello – his last work to include solo flute.

KUHLAU
1786–1832

Daniel Friedrich Kuhlau's compositions for flute were considered 'very fashionable' in elegant Copenhagen society, and were played in the home as well as at concerts.

Kuhlau's father was a military bandsman who sent his fourteen-year-old son to Hamburg for lessons in music theory and composition. While studying in Hamburg, Kuhlau composed his first works for flute and piano. But in 1810 the young composer's studies were interrupted when Napoleon's troops marched into Hamburg. To avoid conscription into the German army Kuhlau fled to Copenhagen, where he lived for the rest of his life, composing and performing.

During his composing career Kuhlau wrote many sets of 'variations' on folk tunes and themes by other composers. In 1824 he wrote a set of variations for flute and piano, using a theme from Weber's opera *Jessonda*. In 1829, perhaps with

Emperor Napoleon in 1807. Kuhlau escaped to Copenhagen when Napoleon invaded Hamburg.

Left: *Copenhagen in the early nineteenth century, as it would have appeared to Kuhlau when he fled there from Germany in 1810.*

Throughout his life Kuhlau was interested in folk music, often using folk songs and dance music in his works.

thoughts of markets abroad, he published two sets of flute variations on Scottish and Irish themes.

Many of Kuhlau's flute works are for an unaccompanied instrument. The composer wrote his first work in this style, three concert duets, in 1813. Later, he wrote further duets, trios, and a 'Grand Quartet' for four flutes. Many of his flute pieces include the word 'grand' in their title, indicating that they are suitable for concert performance.

Kuhlau wrote many flute works as a result of commissions, and such commissions were a valuable source of income to him. Surprisingly though, he did not play the flute himself.

In the last year of his life a fire completely destroyed all Kuhlau's unpublished manuscripts and as a result of the fire he developed a bronchial condition. This illness led to his early death at the age of forty-six.

Military bands played a significant part in Kuhlau's early life through his father's professional associations.

ON THE CD
Sonata in E minor Op. 71
I. Allegro con energia

The Sonata in E minor was published in Bonn in 1825. Although living permanently abroad, Kuhlau held on to his publishing ties in his native Germany. The sonata was written when Kuhlau was at the height of his popularity, and in demand both as a composer and teacher.

DEBUSSY
1862–1918

The flute features often in Claude Achille Debussy's works because its soft mellow tone suits the gentle and flowing style of much of the composer's music.

The Paris Conservatoire, one of the most influential music academies in the world, where Debussy spent his student days.

The Villa Medici in Rome. Debussy, in a white jacket, is in the middle sitting on the last but one step.

When Debussy entered the Paris Conservatoire as a young student of eleven, he had set his hopes on being a concert pianist. But as his studies progressed he found himself turning more towards composition.

Debussy's compositions began an entirely new style in music, which described moods and feelings rather than straightforward scenes and subjects. This style became known as Impressionism, because it aimed to create an impression of a scene, rather than simply trying to describe it.

In 1892 he began work on an orchestral work, based on a poem by Stéphane Mallarmé, which was to bring Debussy's name to the forefront of French music – *L'après-midi d'un faune* ('The afternoon of a faun'). Debussy planned three

A design for the set of Diaghilev's ballet L'après-midi d'un faune, *using the music of Debussy's most well-known work.*

movements, but only completed one, which he called *Prélude*. In mythology the faun is a forest god, with human body and goat's legs. In Debussy's music the animal is represented by the flute. The liquid sounds of the instrument match perfectly the poem's description of a hot summer's afternoon.

The flute remained a popular orchestral instrument for Debussy throughout his composing life, and he included it (and often the piccolo) in all his most important orchestral compositions. He used it to express bright as well as melancholy music. In his opera *Pelléas et Mélisande* the atmosphere is gloomy and dark. Debussy uses three flutes in this work to help evoke the sombre mood. The opera ends with the flutes playing a low quiet chord.

Several of Debussy's works remain unfinished, or left as a single movement. One such flute piece, written in 1913, is entitled *Syrinx*, written for solo flute without accompaniment. The melody of the piece rises and falls in short steps, recreating the breathy playing of the panpipes.

The character Mélisande from Debussy's opera Pelléas et Mélisande. *The work makes important use of the flute.*

ON THE CD
Sonata for flute, viola and harp
III. Finale:
Allegro moderato ma risoluto

Debussy had planned a series of six sonatas, but like so many of his projects it was left unfinished at his death. This sonata was written during the First World War when Debussy had left Paris to live near Dieppe. On hearing the music performed he described it as 'gloomy', yet to modern ears it is a delightful work.

GREAT PLAYERS – EARLY

FRANÇOIS DEVIENNE
1759–1803

François Devienne played both the flute and bassoon expertly. At the age of twenty he joined the orchestra of the Paris Opéra as a bassoonist, while studying the flute with the orchestra's principal flautist. In 1790 Devienne joined the band of the Paris National Guard, later renamed the Paris Conservatoire, where his duties included teaching.

In 1794 he published a tutor for the flute, which illustrates among other things the performing practices of the period.

FREDERICK THE GREAT
OF PRUSSIA 1712–1786

King Friedrich Wilhelm I disapproved of his son Frederick's growing interest in music and the arts, but allowed the young prince music lessons with the flautist and composer Johann Quantz.

After his father's death in 1740, Frederick invited the best musicians of the day to join his court and instituted regular concerts and operas. By now he was a fine flautist as well as an acceptable composer. Concerts were held every evening, often of his own works, and in the space of a very few years Frederick's court at the Palace of Potsdam had become one of the most musical in Europe.

TEBALDO MONZANI
1762–1839

Although born an Italian, Tebaldo Monzani made his permanent home in England and soon became well-known as a solo and orchestral performer, playing a one-keyed Italian flute. In 1797 he established a flute-making business, introducing many improvements to the one-keyed flute.

Monzani also composed many works for flute, which he distributed through his own publishing company. In 1815, he formed a partnership with the publisher and instrument maker Henry Hill. Monzani and Hill became the music seller to the Prince Regent. Like many other great flautists, Monzani incorporated his personal ideas on flute playing into a successful flute tutor.

GREAT PLAYERS – EARLY

ANTOINE REICHA
1770-1836

Antoine Reicha was born in Prague, Czechoslovakia, and began learning the violin and flute with his uncle, Josef Reicha. When the family moved to Bonn, Reicha played in the court chapel, where he met the young Beethoven. In 1801 he moved to Vienna, and became friends with Haydn. Like many performers, Reicha was also a composer, and was well-known for his wind music, and his flute compositions.

In his later years he taught at the Paris Conservatoire, where his pupils included Berlioz and Liszt.

CHARLES NICHOLSON
1795-1837

The English flautist Charles Nicholson was a man of considerable stature, which allowed him to perform on an extra large flute with wide finger holes and embouchure, and so to produce a tone of considerable strength. His flute was built to a design by his father, Charles Nicholson the elder, also a virtuoso flautist.

In 1822 London's Royal Academy of Music opened, and Nicholson was appointed a professor of the flute. In his lifetime, he played in most of the theatre orchestras in London. For the last five years of his life he was principal flautist at Covent Garden.

PAUL TAFFENAL
1844-1908

By the age of ten Paul Taffanel was already playing the flute in public, encouraged by his father, a professional music teacher. He later attended the Paris Conservatoire, where he embarked on a professional career. He played the flute at the Opéra Comique, and later the Opéra, where in 1870 he was promoted to first flute.

Taffanel is regarded as the father of the modern school of French flute playing. In 1879 he formed a society of wind players, which influenced flute playing throughout Europe.

GREAT PLAYERS – MODERN

MARCEL MOYSE
1889–1984

The French flautist Marcel Moyse studied at the Paris Conservatoire, and became solo flautist for the Opéra Comique in 1913, a position he held for twenty-five years. He also played in a variety of other orchestras, and under such world-famous conductors as Toscanini and Klemperer.

He made many recordings, winning a prize in 1928 for his recording of Mozart's D major flute concerto. In 1933 he formed the Moyse Trio with his son and daughter-in-law. The trio made successful recordings and toured extensively.

JEAN-PIERRE RAMPAL
born 1922

Jean-Pierre Rampal first studied the flute with his father, and was later a pupil at the Paris Conservatoire. His first professional position was as solo flautist with the Vichy Opéra orchestra in 1946, and from 1956–62 he was first flautist with the Paris Opéra.

Rampal has always been a keen chamber music player, and founded two chamber groups – the Quintette à Vent Française and the Ensemble Baroque de Paris. His interest is chiefly in the composers of the eighteenth century and in the authentic performance of their flute music.

AURÈLE NICOLET
born 1926

The Swiss flautist Aurèle Nicolet studied the flute in Zurich, and at the Paris Conservatoire under Marcel Moyse. In 1948 he won the flute prize in the Geneva International Music Competition. In 1950 he was engaged as solo flautist in the Berlin Philharmonic Orchestra. From 1953–65 he taught at the Berlin Hochschule für Musik, and in Freiburg.

Nicolet has made many fine recordings, especially of works by Mozart and Bach. Many contemporary composers, such as the Japanese composer Tōru Takemitsu, have written works for him.

GREAT PLAYERS – MODERN

WILLIAM BENNETT
born 1936

William Bennett was born in London and studied the flute at London's Guildhall School of Music. In Paris he studied with Jean-Pierre Rampal. His first professional appointment was with the BBC Northern Symphony Orchestra, and he later played with the London Symphony Orchestra and the Royal Philharmonic Orchestra. Following Aurèle Nicolet, he was Professor at Freiburg Musikhochschule.

He is currently principal flautist with the English Chamber Orchestra with whom he has recently made extensive recordings of solo and chamber music, both baroque and contemporary.

JAMES GALWAY
born 1939

The Irish flautist James Galway learned the violin, only later taking lessons on the flute. He studied first in London, and then at the Paris Conservatoire with Jean-Pierre Rampal. His first professional job was with the Royal Shakespeare Theatre and later he was appointed principal player of the London Symphony Orchestra. He moved to the Royal Philharmonic Orchestra, and finally in 1969 he was engaged as principal flautist of the Berlin Philharmonic.

In 1975 James Galway left orchestral playing to pursue a solo career; success and fame came quickly. James Galway plays an 18-carat gold flute.

RANSOM WILSON
born 1951

Ransom Wilson is widely regarded as one of the most gifted flautists of his generation. He was born in the USA and later studied with Jean-Pierre Rampal in Paris. He studied conducting with several eminent musicians, and received extensive coaching from Leonard Bernstein.

He is currently music director and principal conductor of Solisti New York, a chamber orchestra which he founded in 1981 with the aim of programming contemporary music alongside classical repertoire.

CD Track Listings

Figures in [...] identify the track numbers from the EMI recording. Track lengths are listed in minutes and seconds

EMI is one of the world's leading classical music companies with a rich heritage and reputation for producing great and often definitive recordings performed by the world's greatest artists. As a result of this long and accomplished recording history, EMI has an exceptional catalogue of classical recordings, exceptional in both quality and quantity. It is from this catalogue that EMI have selected the recordings detailed in the track listing below. Many of the recordings featured are available on CD and cassette from EMI.

Antonio Vivaldi 1678–1741
Flute Concerto in G minor ('La notte') Op. 10 No. 2
[1]	I. Largo – Presto (Fantasmi)	4.17
[2]	II. Presto	1.04
[3]	III. Largo (Il sonno)	1.30
[4]	IV. Allegro	2.24

William Bennett (flute) English Chamber Orchestra directed by George Malcolm (harpsichord) Ⓟ1986+

Georg Philipp Telemann 1681–1767
Suite in A minor for flute and string orchestra
[5]	Air à l'italienne	4.13
[6]	Réjouissance	2.44

Elaine Shaffer (flute) Philharmonia Orchestra conducted by Yehudi Menuhin Ⓟ1963/DRM 1994*

Johann Sebastian Bach 1685–1750
Orchestral Suite No. 2 in B minor BWV1067
[7]	Badinerie	1.28

Elaine Shaffer (flute) Bath Festival Orchestra conducted by Yehudi Menuhin Ⓟ1961/1994*

George Frideric Handel 1685–1759
Concerto Grosso in G Op. 3 No. 3
[8]	I. Largo e staccato	0.25
[9]	II. Allegro	2.35
[10]	III. Adagio	0.59
[11]	IV. Allegro	3.35

Hans-Martin Linde (flute) Linde Consort directed by Hans-Martin Linde Ⓟ1985#

Johann Joachim Quantz 1697–1773
Concerto in E minor for flute and string orchestra
[12]	II. Affettuoso	4.16

Karlheinz Zöller (flute) Wolfgang Meyer (harpsichord) Berlin Philharmonic Orchestra conducted by Hans von Benda Ⓟ1961/1990†*

Johann Christian Bach 1735–1782
Quintet in D for flute, oboe, violin viola and cello
Op. 11 No. 6
[13]	I. Allegro	5.15
[14]	II. Andantino	3.23
[15]	III. Allegro assai	2.51

Karlheinz Zöller (flute) Lothar Koch (oboe) Thomas Brandis (violin) Siegbert Ueberschaer (viola) Wolfgang Boettcher (cello) Ⓟ1964/1995†*

Carl Stamitz 1745–1801
Flute Concerto in G Op. 29
[16]	I. Allegro	8.38

Karlheinz Zöller (flute) Berlin Philharmonic Soloists directed by Karlheinz Zöller Ⓟ1966/1995†*

Wolfgang Amadeus Mozart 1756–1791
Concerto in C for flute and harp K299
[17]	II. Andantino	9.15

Elaine Shaffer (flute) Marilyn Costello (harp) Philharmonia Orchestra conducted by Yehudi Menuhin Ⓟ1964/1990*

Friedrich Kuhlau 1786–1832
Sonata in E minor Op. 71
[18]	I. Allegro con energia	8.02

Elaine Shaffer (flute) Hephzibah Menuhin (piano) Ⓟ1972/1995*

Claude Debussy 1862–1918
Sonata for flute, viola and harp
[19]	III. Finale: Allegro moderato ma risoluto	4.46

Michel Debost (flute) Yehudi Menuhin (viola) Lili Laskine (harp) Ⓟ1976/1991§*

72.26
[DDD/*ADD]

Acknowledgements

Macmillan Children's Books would like to thank the following for their permission to use illustrative material reproduced in this book:

a= above, b=below, c=centre, r=right, l=left

AKG, London: 3*b*, 14*l* & *r*, 22*l*, 23*b*, 24*b*, 25*a,br* (and music throughout in panels, and Index) & *bl*, 26*a,b* & *l*, 27*a* &*br*, 28*a*, 29*l*, 30*br*, 31*c*, 33*r*, 34*r*, 35*b*, 36*al* &*r*, 37*b*, 40*al*, 42*l*; **Bridgeman Art Library:** 3*a*, 13*r* (private collection), 23*a* (private collection), 24*a* (private collection), 28*bl* (Museum of London), 29*r* (Fitzwilliam Museum, Cambridge), 30*bl* (Chateau de Versailles/Giraudon), 31*a* (Staatliche Schlosser und Garten, Potsdam), 38*bl* (Christie's, London), 38*r* (Chateau de Versailles/Giraudon), 39*b* & 40*bl* (Musée de la Ville de Paris, Musée Carnavalet/ Giraudon, © SPADEM, Paris 1996), 41*a* (Musée National d'Art Modern, Paris); **English Chamber Orchestra:** 45*l*; **E.T. Archive;** 32*a*, 33*a*, 36*bl*, 39*a*; **Mary Evans Picture Library:** 34*bl*; **The New Grove Dictionary of Music:** 12, 13*l*, 15, 34*a*, 35*al*; **Just Flutes, London:** 7; **Lebrecht Collection:** 11*a* (Andre Lecoz), 11*c* & *b* (Nigel Luckhurst), 13*b*, 22*c* & *r*, 23*r*, 25*r*, 26*r*, 27*l*, 28*r*, 30*a*, 31*b*, 32*b*, 33*bl*, 35*ar*, 37*a*, 38*al*, 40*r*, 41*b*, 43*l* & *r*, 44*l*; **Performing Arts Library:** 6*al* & *r* (Clive Barda), 6*b* (James McCormick), 10*a* & front flap (Jonathan Fisher), 10*b* (Clive Barda), 44*c* (Clive Barda), 45*c* (Clive Barda); **Pitt Rivers Museum:** 8*l*, *a* & *r*, 9*a*, *r* & *b*; **Evelyn Richter:** 44*r*; **Royal College of Music, London:** 42*r*, 43*c*; **Christian Steiner/Angel/EMI Records (NY) Ltd:** 45*r*.

Front cover photograph by Michael Banks (and panel photographs used on pages 1–5, 12, 15, 47). Back cover: *The Concert* by the master of the Female Half Lengths: Bridgeman Art Library; portrait of Mozart: AKG London.

Photographs on pages 16–21 by Phil Rudge.
Map on pages 8–9 by Bill Gregory.
Endpapers: score from Beethoven's Concerto No. 5 ('Emperor') reproduced with permission from Eulenberg Editions Ltd.

The publishers are also grateful to:
EMI Records UK for their cooperation and expertise in compiling the CD.
Harry Seeley and The Flutemakers Guild Ltd for photographs taken at the workshop on pages 16–19, and also the flute featured on the back cover.
Kamera Kids for the model used on pages 16, 20–1.
The Kensington Music Shop for the instrument used on pages 16, 20–1.
Dr Hélène La Rue of the Pitt Rivers Museum, Oxford, for her help in providing the photographs used on pages 8–9.

Every attempt has been made to trace copyright holders. The publishers would be grateful to hear from any copyright holder not acknowledged here.

Index

all musical works appear in italics

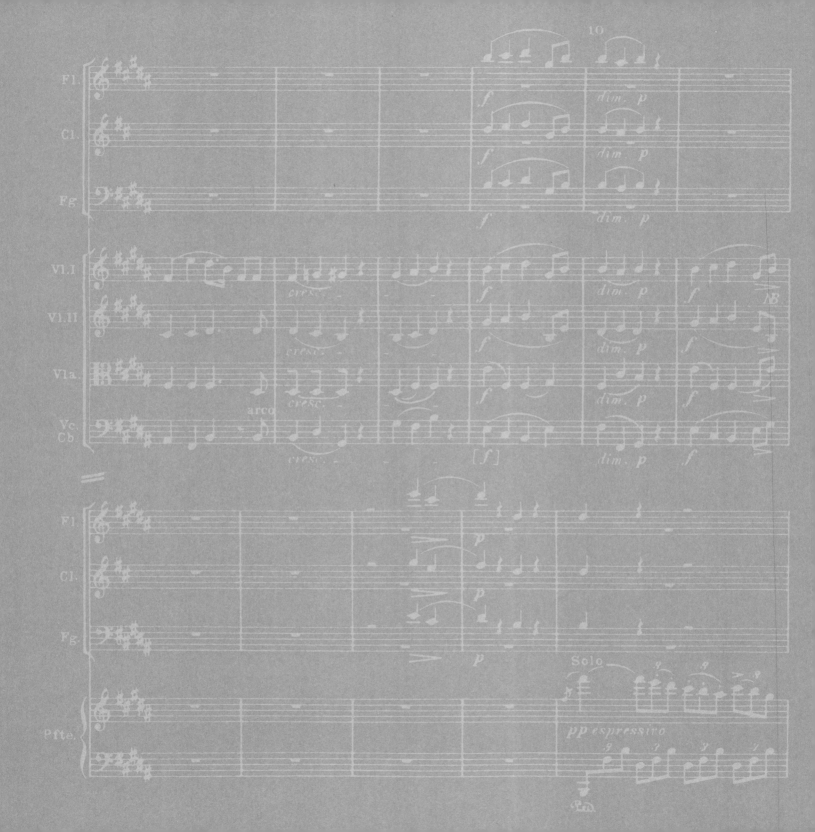